FREESTYLE 2018 SLOW COOKER COOKBOOK

Ultimate Freestyle 2018 Slow Cooker Cookbook

HELEN YOTHERS

CONTENT

CONTENT

CONTENT

Dinner Recipes   144

CONTENT

WEIGHT WATCHERS INTRODUCTION

HOW DOES WEIGHT WATCHERS FREESTYLE PROGRAM WORK?

No need to make your diet and weight loss goals a hectic task. Weighing every ingredient and counting calories can seem pretty difficult. But the Weight Watchers Program is a suitable choice to resolve all the complexities of losing weight.

Backed by online support, this weight loss program allows you to include all kinds of food items in your diet. You can simply monitor your food's nutritional value by utilizing the SmartPoint system offered under the program.

By this way, it becomes easier to decide the size, calories, and the nutritional properties in your daily meals. And it all comes with the freedom to have all kinds of food items you like to have on a daily basis. The Freestyle SmartPoints help in controlling the size of the meals.

In the basic version of the program, the SmartPoint method was introduced. Under this method, all the users get a decided budget of SmartPoints, depending on a variety of factors such as weight, age, gender, height, and others.

The point budget allows a user to track the portions of meals on a daily and weekly basis in order to reduce body weight. The same method is applied in the new freestyle version of the Weight Watchers Program. The upgraded version of the WW Program also includes the system of points.

However, the new version is more flexible in terms of the choices of food items as well as the number of zero point food.

The new list of zero point includes 200 kinds of food choices. Also, the concept of point rollover has been introduced in the Freestyle Program as well. The rollover allows a user to secure some SmartPoints on a daily basis and utilize them at the end of the week. In the basic version of the WW, there were only fruits and vegetables in the category of zero points.

Now, you are able to have certain types of chicken, lentils, beans, and seafood as well.

The freestyle WW Program offers more flexibility in terms of food choices and allows the users to manage the food quantity according to their point budget. Users are now capable of including eggs, turkey, chicken, lentils, and beans without worrying about the point budget.

A user of the WW Program just needs to stay within the range of Freestyle SmartPoints allowed. With that approach, you are open to having all kinds of food of your choice.

So, if you want to eat a cake slice after your lunch, make sure your dinner can cover the used SmartPoints. Hence, your daily and weekly diets become convenient to manage.

Freestyle WW Program is more about controlling your calories. All SmartPoints are allocated to different food items according to their nutritional compositions. Hence, you can reduce your weight without harming the nutrition of your body.

Even with all the assistance of the SmartPoints, the ultimate weight loss approach always stays in your hands. You are the one controlling the diet and food choices. And the same goes for the rollover points you earn.

There is no necessity to use those points. If you can manage yourself effectively, the WW Program can turn you into the best physical version of yourself.

If you look at the overall picture, this program is convenient, affordable, and smoother than other dietary approaches. Understanding the SmartPoints doesn't take too long.

Then, you can shop the right food and ingredients and cook according to the freestyle points. At the same time, you can decide whether to follow a vegetarian diet, a vegan diet, or a non-vegetarian diet, according to your own food preferences.

CHANGES TO DAILY POINTS ALLOWANCE

There are certain changes in the daily point allowance due to the additions to the zero SmartPoint list. The additional 200 food choices in the zero point make the recalculation of the daily allowance important.

The approach of point budget calculation is still similar to the old method. You are required to include your body weight, height, gender, as well as the age. This will help in the calculation of allowed points daily.

19

The users of the old WW Program will find some changes in their daily points allowance. For instance, if you used to get 30 points in a day, it will become 23 SmartPoints within the new program.

But no need to worry about the point reduction, as they are covered by the increased number of food options in the zero point category.

The new version of the program still utilizes the SmartPoints method. The freestyle version has all kinds of foods which you can utilize according to the allocated points.

The calculation of SmartPoints informs about the calories, fat, protein, and other kinds of nutritional values available in multiple food items.

The calculation of SmartPoints informs about the calories, fat, protein, and other kinds of nutritional values available in multiple food items.

Despite the change in the daily points allowance, there is no deflection in the weekly point allowance within the freestyle WW Program.

NEW ZERO POINTS FOOD

The old WW Program contained only two food categories in the zero SmartPoints list. Those categories were fruits and vegetables.

But that has changed in the new freestyle WW version. Now, there are 200+ food choices offered for free, without any expense of SmartPoints.

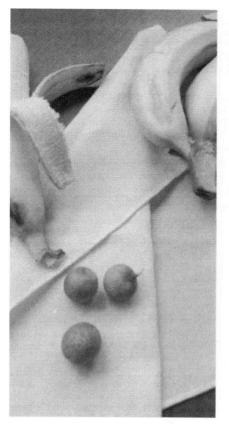

That is why you are now able to include new food items without any expense of SmartPoints.

That is why you are now able to include new food items without increasing the point budget provided for a day.

Here is a list of most food categories that are now a part of zero SmartPoint list in the freestyle WW Program:

1. FRUITS

The new freestyle version has kept the fruits within the zero point allowance. This category includes all kinds of fruits including the canned ones. But the canned fruits can't have any flavors or added sugar.

2. VEGETABLES

You can choose fresh as well as frozen kinds of veggies without using any Freestyle SmartPoints. Thanks to the old and the new zero point collection of the program, you can include all kinds of vegetables in your meals.

However, the zero point vegetable category doesn't include sweet potatoes, avocados, potatoes, and olives.

3. PEAS

Peas are a new inclusion in the collection of zero SmartPoints foods. The freestyle WW Program allows you to have split peas, chickpeas, black-eyed peas, sugar snap, and different other kinds of peas for free.

4. BEANS

The collection of new zero point food includes beans too. This means that you can have kidney beans, edamame, black beans, pinto, bean sprouts, and soybeans along with all other kinds without losing any allocated SmartPoints. This collection also allows you to utilize the refried beans as well as the fat-free kinds of the packaged beans.

5. CORN

Corn choices are now free from the SmartPoints. They are now a part of the zero point collection, which includes all categories of corn such as the sweet corn, baby corn, and cob corn as well.

6. TURKEY BREAST

Turkey breast contains 0 points now, if you get the skinless one. The whole and ground options are allowed. But the ground meat should be free from fat (about 98% fat-free).

7. LENTILS

Lentils have 0 points according to the freestyle version of the WW Program. This includes all kinds of lentils. The nutritional excellence of lentils matches many vegetables; hence, this category has been introduced in the new 0 SmartPoints collection.

8. CHICKEN BREAST

If you pick the skinless breast of chicken, you can save your SmartPoint. The skinless breast of chicken can be in the form of ground meat or you can pick the whole breast. The ground meat, however, needs to contain breast meat type only. Plus, the meat has to be free from fat (about 98% fat-free or more).

9. TOFU

In the new collection of zero point foods, there is tofu as well.

10. EGGS

The eggs are now a part of zero point collection according to the new Freestyle Program. You can include a whole egg or choose egg whites in your meals without losing any SmartPoint.

11. **PLAIN YOGURT**

Plain yogurt, which doesn't contain any fat, is now free from SmartPoints. The category allows you to have traditional yogurt along with other kinds such as the Greek yogurt, soy, or Icelandic yogurt. However, the selected yogurt should have no fat and no sugar or flavoring of any kind.

12. **FISH AND SHELLFISH**

Major fish varieties and shellfishes are in the collection of 0 points now. The Freestyle Program allows you to have fish in the diet for free if it is skinless. You are allowed to have fresh, canned, smoked, and even the frozen category of shellfishes and fishes. Just make sure that those are skinless and have no added sugar or any kind of fat.

So, now that you understand all about the Freestyle Weight Watchers Program and its new zero point allowance. Let's go through some great recipes to make dieting delicious for you!

BREAKFAST RECIPES

BEANS AND CHICKEN BREAST SOUP

BEANS AND CHICKEN BREAST SOUP

GENERAL INFO

Freestyle Smartpoints: 0
Serving Size: 1 ½ Cups
Servings Per Recipe: 6
Calories: 306
Cooking Time: About 4 Hours
And 7 Minutes

NUTRITION INFO

Carbohydrate—44 g
Protein—28 g
Fat—3 g
Sodium—573 mg
Cholesterol—37 mg

INGREDIENTS

Onion—1, chopped
Chicken breast—1 lb., skinless, boneless
Pinto beans—14.5 oz, pick canned and drain
Garlic—2 cloves, minced
Corn—1 can of 14.5 oz, drained
Black beans—1 can of 14.5 oz, drained
Chicken broth—2 cups, no fat
Diced tomatoes and chilies—1 can of 14.5 oz, do not drain
Taco seasoning—1 ¼ oz

BEANS AND CHICKEN BREAST SOUP

DIRECTIONS

1. Put all the available ingredients in your Crock-Pot and cover the pot.
2. Give this setting about 6–8 hours of cooking.
3. After cooking, take out the chicken and use a fork to shred.
4. Your dish is ready to be served.

Recipe Notes

BEAN VEGETABLE AND BARLEY BOWL

BEAN VEGETABLE AND BARLEY BOWL

GENERAL INFO

Freestyle Smartpoints: 4
Serving Size: About 1 Cup
Servings Per Recipe: 8
Calories: 220
Cooking Time: About 8 Hours
And 12 Minutes

NUTRITION INFO

Carbohydrate—48 g
Protein—9 g
Fat—1 g
Sodium—895 mg
Cholesterol—0 mg

INGREDIENTS

Kidney beans—1 cup, dried
Butternut squash—6 cups,
peeled and chopped
Tomatoes—1 can of 28 oz,
choose fire-roasted, chopped
Barley—½ cup
Onions—1, chopped
Vegetable broth—6 cups
Carrots—2, chopped
Bell pepper—1, green, chopped
Garlic—4 cloves, chopped
Celery—2 ribs, chopped
Ground cumin—2 tsps.
Chili powder—1 tbsp.
Bay leaf—1
Paprika—2 tsps.
Pepper and salt—according to
taste

BEAN VEGETABLE AND BARLEY BOWL

DIRECTIONS

1. Allow the available beans to soak in water for about 8 hours overnight.
2. Put all the ingredients in your Crock-Pot and mix properly.
3. Close and cook for about 7–8 hours keeping the heat on a low setting.
4. Beans will get tender and you can use pepper and salt, according to taste.
5. Mix and serve.

Recipe Notes

BROWN SUGAR CHICKPEAS

BROWN SUGAR CHICKPEAS

GENERAL INFO

Freestyle Smartpoints: 2
Serving Size: About ¾ Cup
Servings Per Recipe: 6
Calories: 309
Cooking Time: About 4 Hours
And 8 Minutes

INGREDIENTS

Onion—½, thinly sliced
Chickpeas—1 can of 36 oz, drained and rinsed
Brown sugar—¼ cup
Soy sauce—1/3 cup, sodium reduced
Vegetable broth—¼ cup
Garlic chili—¼ cup, paste
Ginger—1 tbsp., minced
Garlic—2 cloves, minced

NUTRITION INFO

Carbohydrate—53 g
Protein—14 g
Fat—5 g
Sodium—1360 mg
Cholesterol—0 mg

BROWN SUGAR CHICKPEAS

DIRECTIONS

1. In a large enough bowl, you can mix brown sugar, soy sauce, vegetable broth, garlic chili, ginger, and garlic.
2. In the Crock-Pot, put chickpeas as well as onions and cover it with the mixture prepared previously. Stir mix and cover the lid of the pot.
3. Cook for about 3–4 hours, keeping the heat on a low setting.
4. Your dish is ready to be served.

Recipe Notes

CHEESY CHICKEN LASAGNA

CHEESY CHICKEN LASAGNA

GENERAL INFO

Freestyle Smartpoints: 9
Serving Size: Almost 1 Cup
Servings Per Recipe: 10
Calories: 345
Cooking Time: About 1 Hour
And 25 Minutes

INGREDIENTS

Lasagna noodles—8 oz, don't boil
Marinara sauce—50 oz
Skim mozzarella—2 1/4 cups, shredded and divided
Ricotta cheese—15 oz, fat reduced
Cooked chicken—3 cups, cut into tiny pieces

NUTRITION INFO

Carbohydrate—31 g
Protein—27 g
Fat—11 g
Sodium—797 mg
Cholesterol—64 mg

CHEESY CHICKEN LASAGNA

DIRECTIONS

1. Use the available cooking spray to coat your Crock-Pot.
2. At the bottom of the Crock-Pot, you need to make a layer of marinara sauce (use 1 cup). Then, include a layer of 1/3 part of the lasagna you have. Top this layer with ricotta and include about a cup of mozzarella, sauce, and half of the available chicken pieces. Do the same thing again until the noodles are finished.
3. Cover and let the mixture bake for about 5–6 hours, keeping the heat on low. The edges will start getting bubbly. Then, you can open the pot cover and let the cooking go further for another 25–30 minutes.
4. Your dish is ready to be served.

Recipe Notes

CHEESY QUINOA WITH MUSHROOMS

CHEESY QUINOA WITH MUSHROOMS

GENERAL INFO

Freestyle Smartpoints: 8
Serving Size: About 1 Cup
Servings Per Recipe: 6
Calories: 312
Cooking Time: 4 Hours And 6
Minutes

INGREDIENTS

Uncooked quinoa—2 cups
Vegetable broth—4 cups
Mushrooms—12 oz, sliced
Green onions—4, chopped
Garlic—4 cloves, minced
Cream cheese—4 oz, nonfat
Salt—1 ½ tsps.
Italian seasoning—1 tsp.
Parmesan cheese—½ cup
Pepper—1 tsp.

NUTRITION INFO

Carbohydrate—44 g
Protein—15 g
Fat—9 g
Sodium—463 mg
Cholesterol—17 mg

CHEESY QUINOA WITH MUSHROOMS

DIRECTIONS

1. Apart from the Parmesan cheese, put all ingredients in your Crock-Pot. Stir mix everything.
2. Cover and cook for about 5 hours keeping the Crock-Pot on low setting.
3. Make sure quinoa gets cooked properly and then top with the Parmesan cheese and cover the pot again.
4. Give about 16–17 minutes for the cheese to melt.
5. Your dish is ready to be served.

Recipe Notes

CINNAMON SWEET AND TANGY APPLE

CINNAMON SWEET AND TANGY APPLE

GENERAL INFO

Freestyle Smartpoints: 8
Serving Size: 1/8 Part Of The Recipe
Servings Per Recipe: 8
Calories: 246
Cooking Time: About 4 Hours And 16 Minutes

NUTRITION INFO

Carbohydrate—49 g
Protein—1 g
Fat—6 g
Sodium—9 mg
Cholesterol—15 mg

INGREDIENTS

Apple butter—1 tbsp.
Apples—6 cups
Cornstarch—1 tbsp.
Lemon juice—2 tbsps.
Allspice—½ tsp.
Cinnamon—1 tbsp.
Ground cloves—¼ tsp.
Nutmeg—½ tsp.
Flour of whole wheat—¼ cup
White sugar—¼ cup
Brown sugar—¾ cup
Oats—½ cup, choose old-fashioned
Butter—4 tbsps., cubed

CINNAMON SWEET AND TANGY APPLE

DIRECTIONS

1. Use a small-sized bowl to mix white sugar, cornstarch, ½ tbsp. of the available cinnamon, half of the available cloves, nutmeg, and allspice.
2. Take another large enough bowl to mix flour with the rest of the available ingredients that are oats, brown sugar, allspice, cinnamon, cloves, and nutmeg. Now, include cubes of butter as well and mash everything using your hand.
3. Take out your Crock-Pot and layer the apple pieces at the bottom. Include apple butter, lemon juice, and coat apple pieces properly.
4. Include the previously prepared mixture of cornstarch and properly stir.
5. Top this mixture with the flour mixture and stir mix.
6. Give a cooking period of 3–4 hours allowing the apple to get crispy and tender.
7. Serve some or keep in refrigerator to serve cold.

Recipe Notes

CREAMY MUSHROOMS WITH KALE

CREAMY MUSHROOMS WITH KALE

GENERAL INFO

Freestyle Smartpoints: 3
Serving Size: About ¾ Cup
Servings Per Recipe: 6
Calories: 127
Cooking Time: About 8 Hours
And 13 Minutes

NUTRITION INFO

Carbohydrate—16 g
Protein—7 g
Fat—5 g
Sodium—277 mg
Cholesterol—7 mg

INGREDIENTS

Olive oil—1 tbsp.
Vegetable broth—1 ½ cups
Onion—1, chopped
Fresh mushrooms—2 lbs.
Paprika—1 tsp.
Leek—1, chopped
Garlic—4 cloves
Kale—1 bunch, remove stems
and chop
White wine—¼ cup, dried
Pepper and salt—according to
taste
Parsley—¼ cup
Sour cream—½ cup, choose the
lighter version

CREAMY MUSHROOMS WITH KALE

DIRECTIONS

1. Exclude the available sour cream and put all the other ingredients in your Crock-Pot.
2. Choose a low heat setting to cook for about 7–8 hours.
3. After cooking, include the cream and stir mix properly. Cook this mixture for another 16–17 minutes to get the desired thickness.
4. Include parsley and mix properly.
5. Your dish is ready to be served.

Recipe Notes

GARLIC PEPPER PINTO BEANS

GARLIC PEPPER PINTO BEANS

GENERAL INFO

Freestyle Smartpoints: 0
Serving Size: About 2/3 Cup
Servings Per Recipe: 8
Calories: 129
Cooking Time: About 8 Hours
And 6 Minutes

INGREDIENTS

Onion—1, diced
Pinto beans—1 lb., choose dry ones and rinse
Poblano peppers—2, seed removed and chopped
Garlic—4 cloves, chopped
Salt—1 tsp.
Cumin—½ tbsp.
Water—6 cups
Bay leaves—2

NUTRITION INFO

Carbohydrate—37 g
Protein—14 g
Fat—1 g
Sodium—313 mg
Cholesterol—0 mg

GARLIC PEPPER PINTO BEANS

DIRECTIONS

1. Properly rinse the beans you have, to get rid of the rocks and sand particles.
2. Include the rinsed beans, garlic, onions, cumin, poblano, bay leaves, and salt in your Crock-Pot.
3. Cover this mixture in your pot with water. Make sure the level of water stays above the layer of beans.
4. Close and cook the beans for about 7–8 hours.
5. Take out the soft beans and serve with cilantro garnishing.

Recipe Notes

INDIAN-STYLE SPICY CHICKPEAS

INDIAN-STYLE SPICY CHICKPEAS

GENERAL INFO

Freestyle Smartpoints: 1
Serving Size: About ¾ Cup
Servings Per Recipe: 6
Calories: 262
Cooking Time: About 6 Hours
And 22 Minutes

NUTRITION INFO

Carbohydrate—41 g
Protein—12 g
Fat—7 g
Sodium—745 mg
Cholesterol—5 mg

INGREDIENTS

Onions—2, chopped
Butter—1 tbsp.
Ginger—1 tbsp., minced
Garlic—2 cloves, minced
Coriander—1 tbsp.
Jalapenos—2, seeds removed and chopped
Paprika—2 tsps.
Cumin—2 tsps.
Ground turmeric—1 tsp.
Indian garam masala—2 tsps.
Tomatoes—1 can of 14 oz, juices intact
Chickpeas—1 can of 30 oz, drained and rinsed
Vegetable broth—2/3 cup
Pepper—½ tsp.
Salt—½ tsp.
Lemon—1

INDIAN-STYLE SPICY CHICKPEAS

DIRECTIONS

1. Use a large enough skillet to heat the available butter, keeping the heat medium.
2. Use the heated butter to mildly cook onions for about 11–12 minutes. Include garlic, jalapenos, and ginger and give another 2–3 minutes.
3. After getting the fragrance of the garlic, include cumin, coriander, paprika, turmeric, and garam masala. Give 30 seconds of sautéing, and then, stir mix the tomatoes.
4. One by one, include chickpeas and the cooked ingredients in your Crock-Pot. Don't include the juice of lemon now.

5. Cover and choose a low heat setting to cook chickpeas for about 5–6 hours.
6. Open and adjust pepper and salt after including the juice of one lemon.
7. Your dish is ready to be served.

Recipe Notes

JALAPENO GARLIC BLACK BEANS

JALAPENO GARLIC BLACK BEANS

GENERAL INFO

Freestyle Smartpoints: 0
Serving Size: ½ Cup
Servings Per Recipe: 10
Calories: 140
Cooking Time: About 8 Hours
And 4 Minutes

INGREDIENTS

Onion—1, quartered
Black beans—2 cups, dried
Jalapeno—2, whole
Garlic—4 cloves, skin removed
Salt—1 tsp.
Bay leaf—1

NUTRITION INFO

Carbohydrate—26 g
Protein—9 g
Fat—1 g
Sodium—238 mg
Cholesterol—0 mg

JALAPENO GARLIC BLACK BEANS

DIRECTIONS

1. Mix all the ingredients together in your Crock-Pot. Use water to cover the mixture of beans in your Crock-Pot. Make sure you let the beans completely sink in the water.
2. Cover and give 8 hours of cooking on a low heat setting.
3. Stir and serve.

Recipe Notes

MUSHROOM PEPPERS LENTIL BOWL

MUSHROOM PEPPERS LENTIL BOWL

GENERAL INFO

Freestyle Smartpoints: 0
Serving Size: About 1 Cup
Servings Per Recipe: 6
Calories: 244
Cooking Time: About 4 Hours
And 12 Minutes
s

NUTRITION INFO

Carbohydrate—45 g
Protein—16 g
Fat—1 g
Sodium—851 mg
Cholesterol—0 mg

INGREDIENTS

Onion—1, chopped
Lentils—1 ½ cups
Bell peppers—1, red, chopped
Mushrooms—2 cups, chopped
Bell peppers—2, green, chopped
Vegetable broth—2 cups
Crushed tomatoes—2 ½ cups
Balsamic vinegar—1 tbsp.
Smoked paprika—1 ½ tsps.
Italian seasoning—1 ½ tbsps.
Kosher salt—1 tsp.
Chili powder—1 ½ tsps.
Pepper and salt—according to taste

MUSHROOM PEPPERS LENTIL BOWL

DIRECTIONS

1. Put all the ingredients in your Crock-Pot and properly stir.
2. Choose a high heat setting to cook for about 3–4 hours.
3. You can add some water if the mixture seems too dry.
4. Adjust pepper and salt according to your taste and serve warm.

Recipe Notes

PORK PEAS BROCCOLI BOWL

PORK PEAS BROCCOLI BOWL

GENERAL INFO

Freestyle Smartpoints: 7
Serving Size: 1 Cup
Servings Per Recipe: 8
Calories: 343
Cooking Time: 8 Hours And 30
Minutes

NUTRITION INFO

Carbohydrate—44 g
Protein—32 g
Fat—4 g
Sodium—528 mg
Cholesterol—74 mg

INGREDIENTS

Garlic—3 cloves, minced
Lean pork—2 lbs., tenderloin
Brown sugar—2 tbsps.
Soy sauce—1/3 cup, reduced sodium
Ginger—1 tbsp., freshly chopped
Oyster sauce—1 tbsp.
Sesame oil—1 tsp.
Sriracha—1 tsp.
Carrots—3, peeled and sliced
Broccoli florets—3 cups
Celery—3 stalks, chopped
Carrots—3, peeled and sliced
Bell pepper—1, red, chopped
Snow peas—1 cup
Spaghetti—12 oz

PORK PEAS BROCCOLI BOWL

DIRECTIONS

1. Put the pork in your Crock-Pot.
2. Take a large enough bowl to mix soy sauce, garlic, oyster sauce, sugar, sesame oil, Sriracha, and ginger.
3. Pour the mixture all over the pork in your Crock-Pot. Turn the pork to the other side.
4. Give 6–8 hours of cooking on a low setting.
5. After the completion of cooking the pork, you can remove the pork to a serving plate and make it shredded with large forks. Then, include carrots, broccoli, snow peas, celery, and pepper in the Crock-Pot.
6. Give 14–15 minutes of cooking to make the veggies tender.
7. Follow the directions given in the spaghetti package to cook it.
8. Mix pork, veggies, and spaghetti together and serve.

Recipe Notes

SPINACH HAM AND PEPPER CASSEROLE

SPINACH HAM AND PEPPER CASSEROLE

GENERAL INFO

Freestyle Smartpoints: 5
Serving Size: 1 Slice
Servings Per Recipe: 6
Calories: 220
Cooking Time: 4 Hours And 12 Minutes

INGREDIENTS

Green pepper—1, chopped
Potatoes (hash brown)—10 oz, frozen and defrosted
Lean ham—4 oz, no bones, chopped
Onions—¼ cup, chopped
Cheddar cheese—1 cup, no fat, shredded
Frozen spinach—10 oz, defrosted and drained
Egg whites—6
Skim milk—¼ cup
Eggs—6
Pepper—¼ tsp.
Salt—½ tsp.

NUTRITION INFO

Carbohydrate—14 g
Protein—22 g
Fat—9 g
Sodium—750 mg
Cholesterol—201 mg

SPINACH HAM AND PEPPER CASSEROLE

DIRECTIONS

1. Use a cooking spray to coat your Crock-Pot.
2. In a small-sized bowl, mix together onions, peppers, and potatoes. Place them into the Crock-Pot bottom and use pepper and salt to season.
3. Take another bowl to mix ham and spinach. Use half of this mixture to make a layer on the veggies in the Crock-Pot. Make another layer over this with half of the cheese. Then, create another layer of ham and spinach and include the rest of the cheese all over it.
4. Prepare a mixture of egg whites, salt, eggs, milk, pepper, and salt.
5. Pour the mixture of eggs on the top of everything in your Crock-Pot.
6. Cover and choose a low setting to cook for about 7–8 hours.
7. Your dish is ready to be served.

Recipe Notes

TANGY PORK CARNITAS

TANGY PORK CARNITAS

GENERAL INFO

Freestyle Smartpoints: 5
Serving Size: About 6 Oz
Servings Per Recipe: 6
Calories: 216
Cooking Time: 8 Hours And 10
Minutes

INGREDIENTS

Onion—1/2, diced
Pork shoulder—2 lbs., no bone,
fat removed, blade roast
Chicken broth—¼ cup
Lime juice—1 tbsp.
Orange juice—2 tbsps.
Salt—1 tsp.
Cumin—1 ½ tsps.
Oregano—1 tsp.
Chili powder or ancho chili—1
tsp.
Pepper—½ tsp.

NUTRITION INFO

Carbohydrate—3 g
Protein—29 g
Fat—9 g
Sodium—509 mg
Cholesterol—91 mg

TANGY PORK CARNITAS

DIRECTIONS

1. Make 4–5 large pork pieces and mix it with all the rest of the ingredients. Use your hands to coat the pork pieces properly.
2. Put the coated pork pieces in your Crock-Pot and turn on the slow cooking mode.
3. Give this about 7–8 hours of cooking. You can put the pork at night in your Crock-Pot and get it ready in the morning for breakfast.
4. Use large forks to shred the cooked pork.
5. Layer the shredded pork over your baking dish and shift it to your broiler to broil for about 5–6 minutes on a high setting. This will make your shredded meat crispier.
6. Mix the previously obtained cooking juices and serve.

Recipe Notes

VEGETABLE CHICKPEAS

VEGETABLE CHICKPEAS

GENERAL INFO

Freestyle Smartpoints: 1
Serving Size: About ¾ To 1 Cup
Servings Per Recipe: 6
Calories: 288
Cooking Time: About 4 Hours
And 14 Minutes

NUTRITION INFO

Carbohydrate—42 g
Protein—12 g
Fat—10 g
Sodium—1021 mg
Cholesterol—0 mg

INGREDIENTS

Sweet onion—1, thinly sliced
Olive oil—1 tbsp.
Chickpeas—1 can of 30 oz,
rinsed and drained
Garlic—3 cloves, minced
Red peppers—1 cup, chopped
and roasted
Zucchini—1, chopped
Vegetable broth—1 cup
Olives—1 cup
Oregano—1 tsp.
Capers—1 tbsp.
Dried thyme—1 tsp.
Bay leaf—1
Rosemary—1 tsp.
Lemon—1, juiced
Pepper and salt—according to
taste

VEGETABLE CHICKPEAS

DIRECTIONS

1. Include some olive oil in your sauté pan, keeping it over a high heat. Use the heated oil to mildly cook garlic and onions. This will take about 3–5 minutes only.
2. Shift the cooked mixture of garlic and onion to your Crock-Pot. Also, put all the other ingredients and cover the top lid.
3. Use a low heat setting to cook this mixture for about 3–4 hours.
4. Adjust pepper and salt according to your taste.
5. Pour lemon juice before serving.

Recipe Notes

if you change nothing, nothing will change

ANONYMOUS

LUNCH RECIPES

APPLE HONEY PORK TENDERLOIN

APPLE HONEY PORK TENDERLOIN

GENERAL INFO

Freestyle Smartpoints: 3
Serving Size: About 2/3 Cup
Servings Per Recipe: 6
Calories: 232
Cooking Time: About 6 Hours
And 12 Minutes

INGREDIENTS

Onion—1, thinly sliced
Pork tenderloin—2 lbs., fat trimmed, lean
Mustard—2 tbsps., choose whole grain
Apples—2, thinly sliced
Kosher salt—1 ½ tsps.
Honey—2 tbsps.
Black pepper—½ tsp.

NUTRITION INFO

Carbohydrate—17 g
Protein—32 g
Fat—4 g
Sodium—746 mg
Cholesterol—98 mg

APPLE HONEY PORK TENDERLOIN

DIRECTIONS

1. Coat pepper and salt all over the pork and place right in the middle of your Crock-Pot.
2. Pour honey and mustard all over the pork.
3. Include onion and apple slices.
4. Cover the top lid and let it cook for about 5–6 hours, keeping the heat on a low setting.
5. Remove the lid during the final 20 minutes and let the liquid get thick. Cut slices of the pork and serve.

Recipe Notes

BROWN SUGAR CHICKEN WITH GARLIC AND CHILM

BROWN SUGAR CHICKEN WITH GARLIC AND CHILI

GENERAL INFO

Freestyle Smartpoints: 5
Serving Size: 6 Oz
Servings Per Recipe: 6
Calories: 249
Cooking Time: About 4 Hours
And 12 Minutes

INGREDIENTS

Soy sauce—1/3 cup, sodium reduced
Chicken thighs—2 lbs., skinless, boneless
Garlic chili—¼ cup
Brown sugar—¼ cup
Ginger—1 tbsp., chopped
Garlic—2, minced

NUTRITION INFO

Carbohydrate—14 g
Protein—31 g
Fat—6 g
Sodium—1138 mg
Cholesterol—132 mg

BROWN SUGAR CHICKEN WITH GARLIC AND CHILI

DIRECTIONS

1. In your Crock-Pot, include brown sugar, soy sauce, ginger, garlic, and chili garlic. Mix this properly and include chicken as well.
2. Stir and cover the top lid to cook for about 3–4 hours on a low heat setting.
3. Remove the chicken and use two large forks to shred the cooked chicken.
4. Shift the heat to high in your Crock-Pot and stir cook the cooking juice to make it a thick sauce.
5. Mix the chicken again and serve.

Recipe Notes

CINNAMON PULLED PORK

CINNAMON PULLED PORK

GENERAL INFO

Freestyle Smartpoints: 3
Serving Size: About 2/3 Cup
Servings Per Recipe: 6
Calories: 190
Cooking Time: About 4 Hours
And 12 Minutes

NUTRITION INFO

Carbohydrate—5 g
Protein—33 g
Fat—4 g
Sodium—500 mg
Cholesterol—98 mg

INGREDIENTS

Ancho chili—1 tsp., powdered
Paprika—1 tbsp.
Ground cumin—1 tsp.
Salt—1 tsp.
Pepper—½ tsp.
Oregano—1 tsp.
Coriander—¼ tsp.
Cinnamon—¼ tsp.
Onion—1, diced
Pork tenderloin—2 lbs., extra lean
Chicken broth—1 cup
Garlic—4 cloves, chopped
Apple cider—1 tbsp.

CINNAMON PULLED PORK

DIRECTIONS

1. In a small-sized bowl, combine all the spices with your hands.
2. Use the spice mixture to coat the available pork.
3. Shift the coated pork in your Crock-Pot and layer onions and pour chicken broth along with apple cider.
4. Cover and give 5–6 hours of cooking on a low heat setting.
5. Take out the pork and use forks to shred.
6. Your dish is ready to be served.

Recipe Notes

CREAMY TOMATO SOUP

CREAMY TOMATO SOUP

GENERAL INFO

Freestyle Smartpoints: 3
Serving Size: 1 ½ Cups
Servings Per Recipe: 6
Calories: 133
Cooking Time: About 4 Hours
And 16 Minutes

INGREDIENTS

Celery—4 stalks, chopped
Olive oil—2 tsps.
Onion—1, chopped
Carrots—2, chopped
Chipotle peppers—4 tbsps.
Garlic—2 cloves, minced
Vegetable broth—4 cups
Whole tomatoes—1 can of 28 oz, juices intact
Oregano—1 tsp.
Bay leaf—1
Cumin—¼ tsp.
Coriander—½ tsp.
Nonfat milk—1 ½ cups
Cream cheese—8 tbsps., nonfat
Pepper and salt—according to taste

NUTRITION INFO

Carbohydrate—18 g
Protein—5 g
Fat—5 g
Sodium—1038 mg
Cholesterol—12 mg

CREAMY TOMATO SOUP

DIRECTIONS

1. In a large enough skillet, heat some olive oil, keeping the heat medium. Include carrots, celery, and onion and mildly cook for about 9–10 minutes. This will make those veggies tender. Put chipotle and garlic and give another 1–2 minutes of cooking.
2. In your Crock-Pot, put tomatoes, bay leaf, vegetable broth, oregano, cumin, and coriander. Also, include the sautéed vegetables.
3. Give this setting a cooking time of 4 hours, keeping the heat low.
4. After cooking, make a puree texture by blending properly.
5. Send the smooth mixture to your Crock-Pot again. Include milk and cheese. Give it about 30 minutes of cooking and adjust the pepper and salt.
6. Your dish is ready to be served.

Recipe Notes

CUCUMBER JALAPENO PORK

CUCUMBER JALAPENO PORK

GENERAL INFO

Freestyle Smartpoints: 5
Serving Size: About 2/3 Cup
Servings Per Recipe: 6
Calories: 289
Cooking Time: About 4 Hours
And 13 Minutes

INGREDIENTS

Jalapeno—1, diced
Lean pork—2.5 lbs., tenderloin
Garlic—8 cloves, chopped
Raw ginger—1.5 tbsp., minced
Rice vinegar—¼ cup
Soy sauce—½ cup, sodium reduced
Carrots—1 cup, shredded
Brown sugar—1/3 cup
Cilantro—¼ cup
Cucumber—1, thinly sliced

NUTRITION INFO

Carbohydrate—20 g
Protein—42 g
Fat—4 g
Sodium—827 mg
Cholesterol—123 mg

CUCUMBER JALAPENO PORK

DIRECTIONS

1. Put the pork into your Crock-Pot.
2. Include ginger, jalapeno, soy sauce, garlic, brown sugar, and vinegar as well.
3. Coat the pork properly and cover the top lid of the Crock-Pot.
4. Give this about 3–4 hours of cooking, keeping the heat on a low.
5. During this time, you can cut slices of cucumber and carrots and chop cilantro.
6. Take out the cooked pork, cut into pieces, and serve with the sliced veggies and cilantro.

Recipe Notes

CURRY CHICKEN WITH COCONUT MILK AND BASIL

CURRY CHICKEN WITH COCONUT MILK AND BASIL

GENERAL INFO

Freestyle Smartpoints: 2
Serving Size: About 6 Oz
Servings Per Recipe: 6
Calories: 226
Cooking Time: About 4 Hours
And 12 Minutes

INGREDIENTS

Coconut milk—1 can of 14 oz
Chicken breast—2 lbs., skinless,
boneless
Jalapenos—1, chopped
Ginger—1 tbsp., chopped
Limes—2
Garlic—3 cloves
Turmeric—1 tsp.
Curry powder—1 tsp.
Cumin—1 tsp.
Pepper—½ tsp.
Salt—1 tsp.
Cinnamon—½ tsp.

NUTRITION INFO

Carbohydrate—4 g
Protein—33 g
Fat—6 g
Sodium—479 mg
Cholesterol—74 mg

CURRY CHICKEN WITH COCONUT MILK AND BASIL

DIRECTIONS

1. In your blender, include basil, coconut milk, garlic, jalapeno, ginger, turmeric, lime juice, curry powder, cumin, pepper, cinnamon, and salt. Combine properly.
2. Put the chicken in your Crock-Pot and cover it with the prepared sauce. Close the top lid and let it cook for about 3–4 hours, keeping the heat to high setting.
3. Make sure the chicken gets tender properly. Check the tenderness with a fork or a knife.
4. Serve warm.

Recipe Notes

FLANK STEAK PEPPER BOWL

FLANK STEAK PEPPER BOWL

GENERAL INFO

Freestyle Smartpoints: 5
Serving Size: About 2/3 Cup
Servings Per Recipe: 6
Calories: 257
Cooking Time: About 8 Hours
And 6 Minutes

INGREDIENTS

Green pepper—1
Flank steak—2 lbs., fat removed, lean
Onion—1, thinly sliced
Yellow pepper—1
Bay leaf—1
Garlic—4 cloves, chopped
Cumin—¾ tsp.
Beef broth—¾ cup, no fat
Oregano—¾ tsp.
Salt—¼ tsp.
Tomato paste—3 tbsps.

NUTRITION INFO

Carbohydrate—7 g
Protein—35 g
Fat—10 g
Sodium—311 mg
Cholesterol—104 mg

FLANK STEAK PEPPER BOWL

DIRECTIONS

1. Grease your Crock-Pot using a cooking spray.
2. Include all the ingredients in the pot and mix properly.
3. Close and give about 7–8 hours of cooking on a low heat setting.
4. Make sure you check the tenderness of the meat during the last 40 minutes of cooking.
5. Serve warm.

Recipe Notes

GREEN CHILI CORN SOUP WITH KALE

GREEN CHILI CORN SOUP WITH KALE

GENERAL INFO

Freestyle Smartpoints: 2
Serving Size: 1 Cup
Servings Per Recipe: 6
Calories: 145
Cooking Time: About 4 Hours
And 12 Minutes

NUTRITION INFO

Carbohydrate—32 g
Protein—4 g
Fat—2 g
Sodium—1059 mg
Cholesterol—0 mg

INGREDIENTS

Vegetable broth—4 cups
Roasted tomatoes—1 can of
14.5 oz, fire-roasted and crushed
Green chilies—1 can of 4 oz
Jalapeno—1, seeded and minced
Corn—1 can of 10 oz,
Creamed corn—1 can of 10 oz
Kale—4 cups
Onion—1, minced
Bay leaf—1
Garlic—4 cloves, minced
Oregano—2 tsps.
Cumin—2 tsps.
Chili powder—2 tsps.
Pepper and salt—according to
taste

GREEN CHILI CORN SOUP WITH KALE

DIRECTIONS

1. Include every ingredient in your Crock-Pot.
2. Cover and give it about 4 hours of cooking, keeping the heat on a low setting.
3. Your dish is ready to be served.

Recipe Notes

INDIAN SPICY CHICKEN WITH CAULIFLOWER

INDIAN SPICY CHICKEN WITH CAULIFLOWER

GENERAL INFO

Freestyle Smartpoints: 5
Serving Size: About ¾ Cup
Servings Per Recipe: 6
Calories: 289
Cooking Time: About 4 Hours
And 16 Minutes

NUTRITION INFO

Carbohydrate—15 g
Protein—34 g
Fat—9 g
Sodium—1378 mg
Cholesterol—103 mg

INGREDIENTS

Chicken breast—1 lb., skinless, boneless, chopped
Chicken thighs—1 lb., skinless, boneless, chopped
Onion—1, diced
Olive oil—2 tsps.
Ginger—1 tbsp.
Garlic—4 cloves, minced
Garam masala—2 tbsps.
Tomato paste—2 tbsps.
Kosher salt—2 tsps.
Paprika—2 tsps.
Tomatoes—1 can of 28 oz, fire-roasted and crushed
Cayenne pepper—1/8 tsp.
Coconut milk—1 cup, nonfat
Cauliflower florets—3 cups

INDIAN SPICY CHICKEN WITH CAULIFLOWER

DIRECTIONS

1. Take a large enough skillet and warm some olive oil, keeping the medium-high heat. Include onions and let it cook for about 7–8 minutes. As it turns brown, you can include ginger and garlic. Give another minute of cooking, and then, include garam masala, tomato paste, salt, cayenne pepper, and paprika. Stir this mixture for 1–2 minutes over heat.

2. Now, include the cooked spices and onion into your Crock-Pot along with the chicken. Also, add tomatoes and cover the top lid.

3. Cook the chicken for about 3–4 hours, keeping the pot to high heat setting.

4. During the last 30 minutes, include coconut milk and cauliflower florets.

5. Open the lid and stir to get the desired consistency.

6. Your dish is ready to be served.

Recipe Notes

ONION GARLIC BEEF ENCEBOLLADO

ONION GARLIC BEEF ENCEBOLLADO

GENERAL INFO

Freestyle Smart Points: 3
Serving Size: About 6 Oz
Servings Per Recipe: 6
Calories: 215
Cooking Time: About 8 Hours
And 12 Minutes

INGREDIENTS

Onions—2, thinly sliced
Beef roast—2 lbs., top round, extra lean
Beef broth—1 cup
Garlic—4 cloves, thinly sliced
Dried oregano—2 tsps.
White vinegar—2 tbsps.
Pepper and salt—according to taste
Cumin—1 tsp.

NUTRITION INFO

Carbohydrate—5 g
Protein—37 g
Fat—5 g
Sodium—166 mg
Cholesterol—92 mg

ONION GARLIC BEEF ENCEBOLLADO

DIRECTIONS

1. Include the beef in your Crock-Pot and use pepper and salt to season it.
2. Cover the beef with garlic and onions.
3. Mix oregano, cumin, vinegar, and broth. Include this in the pot as well.
4. Close the top lid and set it to cook for about 8 hours, keeping the heat on a low setting.
5. Your dish is ready to be served.

Recipe Notes

PEPPER AND TOMATO CHICKEN

PEPPER AND TOMATO CHICKEN

GENERAL INFO

Freestyle Smartpoints: 0
Serving Size: 2/3 Cup
Servings Per Recipe: 6
Calories: 236
Cooking Time: About 4 Hours
And 6 Minutes

INGREDIENTS

Tomatoes—1 can of 20 oz, fire-roasted and chopped
Chicken breast—2 lbs., skinless, boneless, chopped
Sweet onion—1, cut into slices
Red peppers—3, cut into slices
Balsamic vinegar—2 tbsps.
Garlic—2 cloves, minced
Pepper flakes—1 tsp.
Italian seasoning—1 tbsp.
Salt—1 tsp.
Black pepper—1 tsp.

NUTRITION INFO

Carbohydrate—15 g
Protein—34 g
Fat—2 g
Sodium—670 mg
Cholesterol—74 mg

PEPPER AND TOMATO CHICKEN

DIRECTIONS

1. Place your chicken and all the other ingredients in your Crock-Pot.
2. Cover and let the chicken cook for about 4 hours on a low heat setting.
3. Make sure that the chicken gets tender.
4. Your dish is ready to be served.

Recipe Notes

QUINOA CELERY CHICKEN MEATBALLS

QUINOA CELERY CHICKEN MEATBALLS

GENERAL INFO

Freestyle Smartpoints: 1
Serving Size: 5–6 Meatballs
Servings Per Recipe: 6
Calories: 250
Cooking Time: About 4 Hours
And 32 Minutes

INGREDIENTS

Cooked quinoa—¾ cup
Ground chicken—2 lbs., about 98% lean
Celery—1 rib, chopped
Carrot—1, chopped
Garlic powder—1 tsp.
Egg—1, beaten lightly
Salt—½ tsp.
Onion powder—1 tsp.
Buffalo sauce—1 ½ cups
Pepper—½ tsp.

NUTRITION INFO

Carbohydrate—7 g
Protein—33 g
Fat—9 g
Sodium—538 mg
Cholesterol—138 mg

QUINOA CELERY CHICKEN MEATBALLS

DIRECTIONS

1. Preheat the oven to a temperature of 400°F.
2. Exclude the available buffalo sauce, and mix all the other ingredients to combine.
3. Prepare meatballs with the mixture and layer them on a greased baking sheet.
4. Shift the meatballs into your oven in batches to make them brown a little. This can take up to 6–7 minutes.
5. Now, add half of the available buffalo sauce into your Crock-Pot. Then, place the meatballs in the pot as well. Pour the meatballs with the rest of the sauce.
6. Carefully stir and close the top lid.
7. Give about 3–4 hours of cooking, keeping the heat to a low setting.
8. Your dish is ready to be served.

Recipe Notes

SESAME PORK SHRED FOR TACOS

SESAME PORK SHRED FOR TACOS

GENERAL INFO

Freestyle Smartpoints: 5
Serving Size: About 2/3 Cup
Servings Per Recipe: 8
Calories: 251
Cooking Time: About 8 Hours
And 12 Minutes

INGREDIENTS

Brown sugar—1/3 cup
Pork tenderloin—3 lbs., get lean meat
Garlic—10 cloves, whole
Soy sauce—1/3 cup, sodium reduced
Jalapenos—2, diced
Red onion—½ cup, diced
Rice wine vinegar—1 tbsp.
Ginger root—2 tbsps., peeled and grated
Sesame seeds—2 tbsps.

NUTRITION INFO

Carbohydrate—13 g
Protein—37 g
Fat—5 g
Sodium—449 mg
Cholesterol—111 mg

SESAME PORK SHRED FOR TACOS

DIRECTIONS

1. In a small-sized bowl, mix soy sauce, sugar, jalapenos, red onion, rice vinegar, ginger, and sesame seeds.
2. Place pork as well as garlic in your Crock-Pot. Pour the prepared mixture all over the meat.
3. Cover and cook for about 7–8 hours, keeping the heat on a low setting.
4. Open the lid during the last 25 minutes of cooking. Use a large fork to shred the pork in the Crock-Pot. Stir and leave for open-lid cooking for about 20–30 minutes.
5. Shred the pork more and prepare tacos with cilantro, lime, and equal amount of shredded pork.
6. Your dish is ready to be served.

Recipe Notes

SPICY BEEF TACOS

SPICY BEEF TACOS

GENERAL INFO

Freestyle Smartpoints: 3
Serving Size: About 2/3 Cup Of Cooked Beef
Servings Per Recipe: 8
Calories: 237
Cooking Time: About 9 Hours And 16 Minutes

NUTRITION INFO

Carbohydrate—8 g
Protein—43 g
Fat—7 g
Sodium—163 mg
Cholesterol—104 mg

INGREDIENTS

Ancho chili—2, dried, seeds removed
Chicken broth—2 cups, sodium reduced, boiling
Garlic—4 cloves, minced
Guajillo chili—2, dried, seeds removed
Chipotle chili—4 tbsps.
Onion—1
Oregano—1 tsp.
Cumin—½ tsp.
Coriander—½ tsp.
Pepper and salt—according to taste
Beef roast—3 lbs., top round, extra lean

SPICY BEEF TACOS

DIRECTIONS

1. In a large enough bowl, mix dried chilies with the boiling broth. Stir and cover to rest for about 25–30 minutes.
2. Shift this mixture to your blender along with onion, garlic, oregano, chipotles, cumin, and coriander. Get a smooth blended consistency.
3. Use pepper and salt to coat the beef roast. Put the beef in your Crock-Pot and pour the prepared puree all over it.
4. Cover and give about 8 hours of cooking, keeping the heat low.
5. Open and shred the meat and stir mix before serving in tacos.

Recipe Notes

VEGETABLES AND WORCESTERSHIRE BEEF ROAST

VEGETABLES AND WORCESTERSHIRE BEEF ROAST

GENERAL INFO

Freestyle Smartpoints: 6
Serving Size: About 340 G
Servings Per Recipe: 8
Calories: 331
Cooking Time: About 8 Hours
And 16 Minutes

INGREDIENTS

Carrots—4, chopped
Beef roast—3 lbs., round, extra lean
Onion—1, chopped
Potatoes—2 lbs., chopped
Cornstarch—1 tbsp.
Garlic cloves—3, whole
Worcestershire sauce—2 tbsps.
Cold water—2 tbsps.
Fresh thyme—1 tbsp.
Pepper and salt—according to taste

NUTRITION INFO

Carbohydrate—26 g
Protein—42 g
Fat—7 g
Sodium—160 mg
Cholesterol—99 mg

VEGETABLES AND WORCESTERSHIRE BEEF ROAST

DIRECTIONS

1. First of all, include cold water and cornstarch in your Crock-Pot.
2. Include carrots, potatoes, garlic, and onion in your Crock-Pot as well. Use pepper and salt to season the veggies.
3. Also, use some more pepper and salt to coat the beef roast. Shift this beef into the Crock-Pot, right in the middle of the vegetables.
4. Cover the meat with Worcestershire sauce and cover the top lid.
5. Keeping the heat to low, cook this mixture for about 9–10 hours.
6. Use a knife to slice the beef roast into long pieces.
7. Simmer before serving to get a perfect consistency.

Recipe Notes

you are one workout away from a good mood

ANONYMOUS

DINNER RECIPES

BACON AND PINTO BEANS

BACON AND PINTO BEANS

GENERAL INFO

Freestyle Smartpoints: 1
Serving Size: About 2/3 Cup
Servings Per Recipe: 10
Calories: 186
Cooking Time: About 8 Hours
And 12 Minutes

NUTRITION INFO

Carbohydrate—33 g
Protein—16 g
Fat—7 g
Sodium—387 mg
Cholesterol—8 mg

INGREDIENTS

Onion—1, diced
Pinto beans—1 lb., dried, rinsed, and sorted
Garlic—3 cloves, chopped
Jalapenos—2, diced and seeds removed
Bacon—4 pieces
Tomatoes—3, chopped
Cumin—1 tbsp.
Green pepper—1, chopped
Dried oregano—1 tsp.
Salt—1 tsp.
Chicken broth—6 cups, sodium reduced, boiling
Cilantro—¼ cup

BACON AND PINTO BEANS

DIRECTIONS

1. Cut pieces of the available bacon and give it 2–3 minutes of mild cooking in a large enough pan. This will make them crispy.
2. In your Crock-Pot, include onions, beans, pepper, jalapenos, garlic, tomatoes, cumin, salt, and oregano.
3. Pour the boiling broth in the Crock-Pot as well.
4. Include bacon along with the cooking juices collected in the pan. Stir mix and close the top lid.
5. Give about 7–8 hours of cooking on a low heat setting.
6. Your dish is ready to be served.

Recipe Notes

BBQ TURKEY WITH APPLE AND CHILI

BBQ TURKEY WITH APPLE AND CHILI

GENERAL INFO

Freestyle SmartPoints: 2
Serving Size: about 238 g
Servings per Recipe: 8
Calories: 215
Cooking Time: about 4 hours and 8 minutes

NUTRITION INFO

Carbohydrate—22 g
Protein—25 g
Fat—3 g
Sodium—712 mg
Cholesterol—68 mg

INGREDIENTS

Cumin—1 tsp.
Turkey breast—2 lbs., skinless, boneless
Applesauce—½ cup, no sweetness
Chili powder—1 tsp.
Onion—1, sliced
Apples—2, sliced
Salt—1 tsp.
Garlic cloves—2, minced
BBQ sauce—1 cup
Pepper—½ tsp.
Chicken broth—½ cup, sodium reduced

BBQ TURKEY WITH APPLE AND CHILI

DIRECTIONS

1. Include the turkey, apples, and onion slices in your Crock-Pot.
2. Mix together the cumin, BBQ sauce, applesauce, chili powder, salt, broth, pepper, and garlic.
3. Cover the turkey, apples, and onions with the prepared mixture.
4. Give about 4 hours of cooking, keeping the heat to a low setting.
5. Use forks to shred the cooked turkey and stir mix properly.
6. Your dish is ready to be served.

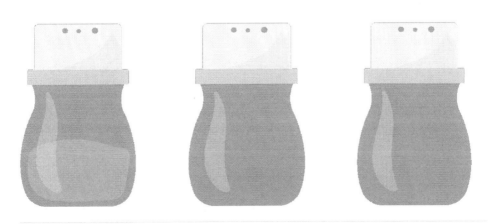

Recipe Notes

CHIPOTLE PEPPER COCOA BEEF STEW

CHIPOTLE PEPPER COCOA BEEF STEW

GENERAL INFO

Freestyle Smartpoints: 5
Serving Size: About ½ Cup
Servings Per Recipe: 8
Calories: 210
Cooking Time: About 3 Hours
And 18 Minutes

INGREDIENTS

Cocoa powder—1 tbsp., no sweetness
All-purpose flour—1/3 cup
Beef brisket—2 lbs., use extra lean, fat trimmed
Ancho chili—1 tbsp., powdered
Salt—½ tsp.
Butter—1 tbsp.
Bell pepper—1 red, 1 green, chopped
Black pepper—¼ tsp., powdered
Diced tomatoes—1 can of 14 oz, undrained
Onion—1, chopped
Chipotle peppers—2 tbsps.
Beef broth—1 ½ cups

NUTRITION INFO

Carbohydrate—10 g
Protein—26 g
Fat—7 g
Sodium—294 mg
Cholesterol—0 mg

CHIPOTLE PEPPER COCOA BEEF STEW

DIRECTIONS

1. Take a small-sized bowl to mix together, flour, cocoa, pepper, salt, and ancho chili. Use some of this mixture as a coating for your beef brisket.
2. Melt some butter in your large enough pan to brown the coated brisket. This will take about 3–4 minutes on both sides.
3. Put the browned meat with all the other ingredients and the mixture of flour prepared before in your Crock-Pot.
4. Close and let it cook for about 5–6 hours on a low heat setting.
5. Use a fork to see if the beef is shredded properly. Shred and simmer for about 10 minutes.
6. Your dish is ready to be served.

Recipe Notes

CROCK-POT BBQ PORK

CROCK-POT BBQ PORK

GENERAL INFO

Freestyle Smartpoints: 2
Serving Size: About 6 Oz
Servings Per Recipe: 6
Calories: 188
Cooking Time: About 8 Hours
And 12 Minutes

INGREDIENTS

Onion—1, slices
Lean pork—2 lbs., tenderloin
Apple cider—1 tbsp.
Chicken broth—½ cup, sodium reduced
Pepper—1 ½ tsps.
Paprika—2 tbsps.
Cumin—1 tsp.
Garlic powder—1 tsp.
Salt—½ tsp.

NUTRITION INFO

Carbohydrate—4 g
Protein—33 g
Fat—4 g
Sodium—286 mg
Cholesterol—98 mg

CROCK-POT BBQ PORK

DIRECTIONS

1. Place the slices of onion in your Crock-Pot. Also, place the pork and include chicken broth in the pot. Mix in the apple cider.
2. Make a mixture of all the spices and use it as a coating for the pork.
3. Close the lid of the Crock-Pot and give this about 8 hours to cook on a low heat setting.
4. Use a fork to shred the cooked meat.
5. Your dish is ready to be served.

Recipe Notes

GROUND TURKEY WITH MUSHROOMS

GROUND TURKEY WITH MUSHROOMS

GENERAL INFO

Freestyle Smartpoints: 3
Serving Size: About ¾ Cup
Servings Per Recipe: 6
Calories: 280
Cooking Time: About 4 Hours
And 12 Minutes

NUTRITION INFO

Carbohydrate—18 g
Protein—36 g
Fat—8 g
Sodium—751 mg
Cholesterol—98 mg

INGREDIENTS

Ground turkey—1 lb., about 99% lean
Ground sausage of turkey—1 lb., choose the lean option
Garlic—4 cloves, minced
Onion—1, chopped
Bell pepper (green)—1, chopped
Bell pepper (red)—1, chopped
Crushed tomatoes—28 oz
Mushrooms—1 cup, chopped
Italian seasoning—1 tbsp.
Tomato paste—¼ cup
Pepper and salt—according to taste

GROUND TURKEY WITH MUSHROOMS

DIRECTIONS

1. Take a large enough skilled for the ground turkey and the turkey sausage. Let the skillet heat for a while, and then, brown the ground meat. Include garlic, onions, and peppers and cook for another 3–4 minutes.
2. Transfer the cooked mixture in your Crock-Pot along with the rest of the ingredients.
3. Cover the top lid and let it cook for about 4 hours, keeping the heat on low.
4. Your dish is ready to be served.

Recipe Notes

HOISIN HONEY PORK COOKED

HOISIN HONEY PORK COOKED IN CHINESE SPICES

GENERAL INFO

Freestyle Smartpoints: 5
Serving Size: About 6 Oz Of Pork
Servings Per Recipe: 6
Calories: 244
Cooking Time: About 8 Hours And 12 Minutes

NUTRITION INFO

Carbohydrate—17 g
Protein—33 g
Fat—5 g
Sodium—695 mg
Cholesterol—99 mg

INGREDIENTS

Hoisin sauce—¼ cup
Soy sauce—¼ cup, sodium reduced
Honey—3 tbsps.
Ketchup—3 tbsps.
Fresh ginger—2 tsps., grated
Garlic—1 clove, minced
Chinese five-spice—½ tsp., powdered
Sesame oil—1 tsp.
Chicken broth—½ cup, sodium reduced
Pork tenderloin—2 lbs., choose lean pork

HOISIN HONEY PORK COOKED IN CHINESE SPICES

DIRECTIONS

1. In a small-sized bowl, mix together all the ingredients apart from the pork tenderloins.
2. Put the pork in your Crock-Pot and use the prepared mixture to pour all over it.
3. Close the top lid of the pot and give about 8 hours of cooking on a low heat setting.
4. Use forks to shred the cooked pork and leave the shredded meat in the mixture for about 20 minutes without closing the lid.
5. Steam some veggies and serve together with the cooked pork.

Recipe Notes

MANGO LIME JERK CHICKEN

MANGO LIME JERK CHICKEN

GENERAL INFO

Freestyle Smartpoints: 4
Serving Size: About 6 Oz
Servings Per Recipe: 6
Calories: 251
Cooking Time: About 4 Hours
And 6 Minutes

NUTRITION INFO

Carbohydrate—19 g
Protein—30 g
Fat—6 g
Sodium—529 mg
Cholesterol—132 mg

INGREDIENTS

Garlic—3 cloves
Chicken thighs—2 lbs., skinless, boneless
Brown sugar—2 tbsps.
Jerk seasoning—2 tbsps.
Pineapple juice—¼ cup
Orange juice—¼ cup
Mango—1, chopped
Lime juice—2 tbsps.
Red onion—2 tbsps., diced
Cilantro—¼ cup
Lime—1, juiced
Pepper and salt—according to taste

MANGO LIME JERK CHICKEN

DIRECTIONS

1. Take a small-sized bowl to mix jerk seasoning, garlic, orange juice, brown sugar, lime juice, and pineapple juice.
2. Place the chicken in your Crock-Pot and use jerk seasoning to coat. Also, put the prepared mixture all over the chicken.
3. Stir and close the top lid of the pot and let it cook for about 4 hours, keeping the heat on low.
4. After cooking, open the lid and use a fork to make the chicken shredded. Stir and leave the shredded chicken in the cooking mixture for about 12–16 minutes.
5. Your dish is ready to be served.

Recipe Notes

MADRAS-STYLE LENTILS

MADRAS-STYLE LENTILS

GENERAL INFO

Freestyle Smartpoints: 3
Serving Size: About ¾ Cup
Servings Per Recipe: 6
Calories: 242
Cooking Time: About 4 Hours
And 12 Minutes

INGREDIENTS

Tomato sauce—3 cups
Lentils—3 cups, choose canned lentils, rinsed and drained
Potatoes—3 cups, peeled and cut into cubes
Onion—1, finely chopped
Coconut milk—¾ cup
Spinach—6 cups
Garlic—4 cloves, minced
Dried oregano—¾ tsp.
Salt—¾ tsp.
Coriander—½ tsp.
Cumin—¾ tsp.
Pepper flakes—½ tsp.
Black pepper—½ tsp.

NUTRITION INFO

Carbohydrate—44 g
Protein—13 g
Fat—3 g
Sodium—1079 mg
Cholesterol—0 mg

MADRAS-STYLE LENTILS

DIRECTIONS

1. Put all the ingredients in your Crock-Pot.
2. Cover the top lid and let the mixture cook for about 4 hours on a low heat setting.
3. After cooking, adjust pepper, salt, and flakes of red pepper according to your taste.
4. Stir mix properly and serve.

Recipe Notes

PEANUT BUTTER CHICKEN WITH SOY SAUCE

PEANUT BUTTER CHICKEN WITH SOY SAUCE

GENERAL INFO

Freestyle Smartpoints: 1
Serving Size: About ¾ Cup
Servings Per Recipe: 6
Calories: 269
Cooking Time: About 4 Hours
And 12 Minutes

NUTRITION INFO

Carbohydrate—14 g
Protein—32 g
Fat—10 g
Sodium—532 mg
Cholesterol—56 mg

INGREDIENTS

Red peppers—2, chopped
Chicken breast—1 ½ lbs.,
skinless, boneless
Peanut butter—½ cup, fat
reduced
Onion—1, diced
Chicken broth—½ cup, sodium
reduced
Lime juice—1 tbsp.
Soy sauce—¼ cup, sodium
reduced
Cumin—½ tbsp.
Coriander—½ tbsp.

PEANUT BUTTER CHICKEN WITH SOY SAUCE

DIRECTIONS

1. Put onions, chicken, and red peppers in your Crock-Pot.
2. Pick a small-sized bowl to mix soy sauce, peanut butter, chicken broth, lime juice, coriander, and cumin.
3. Cover the chicken in the pot with the prepared sauce.
4. Close the top lid and cook the mixture for about 4 hours, keeping the heat to a high setting.
5. After that, use a fork to shred the chicken into small-sized pieces.
6. Use cilantro, lime, and scallions to garnish before serving.

Recipe Notes

PEAR BALSAMIC PORK

PEAR BALSAMIC PORK

GENERAL INFO

Freestyle Smartpoints: 4
Serving Size: About 4 Oz
Servings Per Recipe: 6
Calories: 253
Cooking Time: About 4 Hours
And 8 Minutes

INGREDIENTS

Balsamic vinegar—¼ cup
Pork tenderloin—2 lbs., fat
trimmed, lean
Vegetable broth—½ cup
Honey—2 tbsps.
Worcestershire sauce—1 tbsp.
Garlic—1 clove
Soy sauce—1 tbsp.
Dried rosemary—1 tsp.
Pears—3, slices
Pepper and salt—according to
taste

NUTRITION INFO

Carbohydrate—23 g
Protein—32 g
Fat—4 g
Sodium—340 mg
Cholesterol—98 mg

PEAR BALSAMIC PORK

DIRECTIONS

1. Take a large enough bowl to mix honey, vinegar, broth, soy sauce, Worcestershire sauce, rosemary, and garlic.
2. Use pepper and salt to season the tenderloin and place it in your Crock-Pot. Also, include pears in the Crock-Pot as well.
3. Cover the pork and pears with the prepared mixture.
4. Close and give about 4 hours of cooking on a high heat setting.
5. Cut slices of the pork and leave in the mixture for about 25 minutes before serving.

Recipe Notes

SERRANO CHILI SPICY BEEF ROAST

SERRANO CHILI SPICY BEEF ROAST

GENERAL INFO

Freestyle Smartpoints: 3
Serving Size: About 2/3 Cup
Servings Per Recipe: 8
Calories: 247
Cooking Time: About 8 Hours
And 12 Minutes

NUTRITION INFO

Carbohydrate—6 g
Protein—40 g
Fat—6 g
Sodium—204 mg
Cholesterol—102 mg

INGREDIENTS

Pepper and salt—according to taste
Beef roast—3 lbs., round, lean
Lime juice—4 tbsps.
Worcestershire sauce—2 tbsps.
Onion—1 ½ cups, chopped
Garlic—3 cloves, chopped
Bell pepper—1 cup, red one, chopped
Beef broth—½ cup, no fat
Serrano chili—3, seeds and stems removed and chopped
Dried oregano—½ tsp.
Diced tomatoes—1 cup, use canned tomatoes

SERRANO CHILI SPICY BEEF ROAST

DIRECTIONS

1. Use pepper and salt to coat your beef and transfer it to your Crock-Pot.
2. Use a medium-sized bowl to mix together the beef broth, lime juice, and Worcestershire sauce. Mix properly and pour in the Crock-Pot covering the beef.
3. Close the top lid of the pot and give about 8 hours of cooking, keeping the heat on a low setting.
4. Use large forks to shred the cooked beef and leave the meat in the cooking juice for about 20–40 minutes. Keep the Crock-Pot on a low heat mode during this time.
5. Your dish is ready to be served

Recipe Notes

SLOW COOKED BEEF AND VEGETABLES

SLOW COOKED BEEF AND VEGETABLES

GENERAL INFO

Freestyle Smartpoints: 3
Serving Size: About ½ Cup
Servings Per Recipe: 10
Calories: 224
Cooking Time: About 8 Hours
And 12 Minutes

INGREDIENTS

Celery—1 rib, diced
Leaf beef—2 ½ lbs., fat trimmed, top round
Carrot—1, diced after peeling
Onion—1/2, diced
Garlic—4 cloves, chopped
Crushed tomatoes—1 can of 14.5 oz
Diced tomatoes—1 can of 14.5 oz
Pepper and salt—according to taste
Bay leaves—2
Beef broth—1 ½ cups
Fresh thyme—2 tbsps., chopped
Fresh rosemary—2 tbsps., minced

NUTRITION INFO

Carbohydrate—6 g
Protein—27 g
Fat—9 g
Sodium—241 mg
Cholesterol—78 mg

SLOW COOKED BEEF AND VEGETABLES

DIRECTIONS

1. Place celery, carrots, garlic, and onion pieces in your Crock-Pot.
2. Properly coat the beef with pepper and salt. Include the meet in the Crock-Pot as well.
3. Transfer all the other ingredients in the pot and give it about 7–8 hours of cooking in a low heat.
4. Serve warm with pasta or make burgers or sandwiches.

Recipe Notes

SWEET ONION SOUP

SWEET ONION SOUP

GENERAL INFO

Freestyle Smartpoints: 3
Serving Size: About 1 Cup
Servings Per Recipe: 8
Calories: 111
Cooking Time: About 8 Hours
And 16 Minutes

INGREDIENTS

Butter—2 tbsps.
Sweet onions—4, sliced
Balsamic vinegar—1 tbsp.
Worcestershire sauce—1 tbsp.
Brown sugar—2 tsps.
Garlic cloves—3, minced
Salt—½ tsp.
Pepper—½ tsp.
Vegetable broth—64 oz
All-purpose flour—3 tbsps.
Fresh thyme—2 tbsps.

NUTRITION INFO

Carbohydrate—20 g
Protein—2 g
Fat—3 g
Sodium—1090 mg
Cholesterol—8 mg

SWEET ONION SOUP

DIRECTIONS

1. Put your Crock-Pot in a high heat setting and include the butter, onions, vinegar, Worcestershire sauce, salt, brown sugar, pepper, and garlic. Give about 60 minutes of cooking to get the caramelized texture. You can stir the mixture a few times.
2. Mix the flour and give another 5–6 minutes of cooking.
3. Include thyme and pour the broth in the Crock-Pot.
4. Close the top lid and let it cook for 7–8 hours, keeping the heat to low.
5. Serve with French bread as a topping.

Recipe Notes

TERIYAKI CHICKEN

TERIYAKI CHICKEN

GENERAL INFO

Freestyle Smartpoints: 3
Serving Size: About 6 Oz
Servings Per Recipe: 6
Calories: 229
Cooking Time: About 4 Hours
And 12 Minutes

INGREDIENTS

Minced ginger—1 tbsp.
Chicken breast—2 lbs., skinless, boneless
Fresh pineapple—1 cup, chopped
Teriyaki sauce—1 cup, low-sodium
Soy sauce—¼ cup, low-sodium
Pineapple juice—½ cup
Garlic—2 cloves, chopped

NUTRITION INFO

Carbohydrate—16 g
Protein—36 g
Fat—1 g
Sodium—2496 mg
Cholesterol—74 mg

TERIYAKI CHICKEN

DIRECTIONS

1. At the Crock-Pot bottom, you can put your chicken.
2. Cover the chicken with pineapple pieces.
3. Take a small-sized bowl to mix together teriyaki sauce, ginger, soy sauce, pineapple juice, and garlic.
4. Include the prepared mixture in the Crock-Pot as well.
5. Close and give about 3–4 hours of cooking, keeping the heat on a high setting.
6. Use a large fork to shred the chicken into pieces and give about 25 minutes of stir cooking to get the desired consistency.
7. Your dish is ready to be served.

Recipe Notes

TURKEY CHILI

TURKEY CHILI

GENERAL INFO

Freestyle Smartpoints: 2
Serving Size: 1 ¼ Cups
Servings Per Recipe: 8
Calories: 317
Cooking Time: About 8 Hours
And 26 Minutes

NUTRITION INFO

Carbohydrate—41 g
Protein—29 g
Fat—5 g
Sodium—496 mg
Cholesterol—51 mg

INGREDIENTS

Poblano peppers—2
Tomatillos—1 ½ lbs., removed
from husks and washed
Onion—1, quartered
Jalapenos—3
Turkey breast—1 ½ lbs.,
skinless, boneless
Garlic—8 cloves
Pinto beans—1 can of 20 oz
Hominy—1 can of 28 oz,
drained
Bay leaf—1
Chicken broth—3 cups, sodium
reduced
Cumin—½ tbsp.
Coriander—½ tbsp.

TURKEY CHILI

DIRECTIONS

1. Preheat your oven to 500°F. Then, include a baking sheet layered with poblano, tomatillos, onion, jalapenos, and eight of the available garlic cloves. Put some kosher salt all over and give about 17–20 minutes to roasting. Make sure you shake the ingredients twice or thrice. Set aside and let them cool down. Then, remove seeds and skins from poblano and jalapenos.
2. Shift the roasted ingredients with the collected juice in your blender. Blend to get a smooth salsa.
3. In your Crock-Pot, transfer pinto beans, bay leaf, and hominy. Also, put the turkey in the pot and use coriander, cumin, pepper, and salt to season the turkey and other ingredients in the pot.
4. Cover everything in the Crock-Pot with the prepared salsa and also include chicken broth.
5. Cover and give about 4 hours to cook on a low heat setting.
6. During the last 20 minutes, you can open the pot and use forks to shred the cooked turkey. Stir once and let it cook for the last 20 minutes.
7. Your dish is ready to be served.

Recipe Notes

THANK YOU

Made in the USA
Lexington, KY
11 March 2019